WESTMINSTER ABBEY
THE MONUMENTS

England's finest sculpture collection is scattered round the aisles, chapels and transepts of Westminster Abbey. Yet strangely this is the first guide to devote itself to these magnificent memorials. The selecting and arresting eye of the camera allows us to dwell on individual figures and details without distraction, and brings those in reach which are too high up to enjoy fully.

Since mediaeval times, the Abbey has been the pantheon of national greatness. Elizabeth I and Mary, Queen of Scots, bitter opponents in life, lie in death only yards apart. Gladstone and Disraeli, Canning and Peel posture in the north transept as once they did in the neighbouring Houses of Parliament. The great poets and musicians are here – Shakespeare and Milton, Handel and Purcell. Rubbing cold marmoreal shoulders with these are admirals and aristocrats, generals and deans, now remembered only by their monuments, which are often the finest in the Abbey. The book's biographical captions detail these forgotten lives.

Starting at the main entrance, the visitor is conducted round the Abbey in a clockwise direction. Examples of Mediaeval, Tudor and Victorian work are included but the book concentrates on the 17th and 18th centuries, when monumental sculpture reached its apogee, with artists like Rysbrack, Roubiliac, Nollekens and Flaxman. These noble and poignant works of art make us ponder the most inscrutable of mysteries, Man's relationship with his own death.

Joe Whitlock Blundell's photographs of sculpture, 'Glyptomania', were exhibited at the Royal Photographic Society National Centre of Photography in November 1988. Dr John Physick is a former Deputy Director of the Victoria and Albert Museum and President of the Church Monument Society.

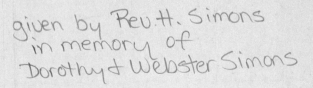

WESTMINSTER ABBEY

PHOTOGRAPHS BY
JOE WHITLOCK BLUNDELL

THE MONUMENTS

INTRODUCTION BY
JOHN PHYSICK

JOHN MURRAY

First published in 1989
by John Murray (Publishers) Ltd
50 Albemarle Street, London W1X 4BD
Designed by Joe Whitlock Blundell
Typeset, printed and bound in Great Britain
by Butler & Tanner Ltd, Frome and London
British Library Cataloguing in Publication Data
Westminster Abbey, the monuments.
1. London. Westminster (London Borough).
Collegiate churches. Westminster Abbey.
Monuments
I. Whitlock Blundell, Joe   731′.76′0942132
ISBN 0-7195-4686-9

CONTENTS

Illustrations in the preliminary pages of the book: Britannia and the Lion [66], sarcophagus supported by red indians [65], putto with wreath from the monument to Hugh Chamberlen by Scheemakers in the north choir aisle, books from the monument to Dr Richard Mead by Scheemakers in the north aisle, snake [1].

ACKNOWLEDGEMENTS

The interior of Westminster Abbey is characteristically crepuscular, though for a short time each morning there are shafts of light across Poets' Corner (witness the hand of History, [58]), and in the evenings there is a corresponding glow in parts of the North Transept. No artificial light has been used for these photographs. In fact the only tampering with reality occurred in the darkroom where sleight-of-hand cleaned Wordsworth's nose [61] and the elephant's trunk [7], both heavily soiled by countless stroking fingers. It is to be hoped that they will soon be given a more authentic clean, that some of Roubiliac's masterpieces may get a dusting, and even that one day some of the many broken fingers will be replaced.

Many thanks are due to the staff at the Abbey for their helpful co-operation, and in particular to Emma St John-Smith who managed things with friendly efficiency; to Jill Waters who wrote the captions and John Physick for his Introduction; to Denys Baker who drew the plan and David Eccles who lettered the back cover; most of all to Roger Hudson, who had the original idea for the book, and has seen it through with enthusiasm and erudition.

P. Scheemakers

INTRODUCTION

Within the Collegiate Church of St Peter, Westminster, there are about 450 monuments, excluding the many grave-slabs, a large number of which have been worn smooth and are now unidentifiable. Some of these monuments are simple tablets, while others are major artistic creations from the medieval period to the present day. Together, they represent the greatest collection of sculptors' work in this country that can be seen anywhere. Westminster Abbey has become the national collection of sculpture in Britain as a result of being used as the national valhalla, where the great, good and heroic are buried or commemorated. It is also the last resting place of many who cannot be considered of any national or even local interest. A boy of seven years is buried beside Darwin and not far from Isaac Newton. Nearby are monuments to teen-aged youths, one of them beneath that to an assassinated Prime Minister. The choice of the great and good appears to have been quite arbitrary. While there are memorials to soldiers and sailors killed during the wars of the 18th and early 19th centuries, Nelson and Wellington are elsewhere; where are Florence Nightingale, or the painters Constable and Turner? This provides a source of bewilderment and curiosity for the millions of visitors who make the pilgrimage to the church each year.

The medieval royal tombs, executed by brilliant craftsmen, are a superb series, especially those with gilded bronze effigies [43]; that of Edward III is considered the first attempt at portraiture in English monumental sculpture. Beside the high altar the tombs of the Earl and Countess of Lancaster, and the Earl of Pembroke, were once brightly coloured; much of the colouring still remains, though faded, in spite of the attempt by a student in 1968 to set one of the monuments alight. In the chapel of St Edmund is the earliest alabaster effigy in the Abbey, of the purest and finest white quality, to John of Eltham (d 1336) [49], and in the same chapel is the effigy of William de Valence (d 1296) on which survive portions of the coloured plates of Limoges enamel with which it was once covered. Because it has always been protected by a screen from predatory hands, his shield is almost complete, displaying the Valence arms with its border of little red birds (martlets).

Nearly all these monuments have suffered dreadful damage during the last three or four hundred years. Some of this destruction is due to the iconoclasm following the Reformation or during the Commonwealth, but a great deal must be due to vandalism and deliberate theft by visitors. In addition, considerable damage has been inflicted by preparations for coronations. Even funerals have had the same result: in 1775, the wooden canopy of Edward I's tomb was torn down and pieces were used as weapons during the funeral service of the Earl of Bath [35]. But in the early years of the Abbey, practically the only interments, and therefore monuments, allowed in the church, were those of members of the royal family and abbots. It was Richard II who broke with this custom, when he insisted (to the affront both of Londoners and the Abbey community), that John de Waltham, Bishop of Salisbury, be buried in Edward the Confessor's chapel in 1395.

In 1400, Geoffrey Chaucer had been buried in the south transept. His burial there was perhaps because he lived nearby and was not only an official of the royal household, but was also the brother-in-law of John of Gaunt. His Purbeck marble monument, around which has developed the Poets' Corner, was not erected until 1556, and it is probable that it was bought, 'second-hand', from another monastic church which had been demolished after the Dissolution of the Monasteries.

Early in the 16th century, the Italian sculptor, Pietro Torrigiano, was commissioned to create the two outstanding monuments with gilded bronze effigies, to Henry VII and Elizabeth of York [44], and to Lady Margaret Beaufort, the King's mother. While that to Lady Margaret Beaufort still has much of the medieval mood about it, that to Henry VII brought into the Abbey what has been described as the 'finest Renaissance tomb north of the Alps'.

In 1540 the Abbey was dissolved and for ten years the church became a cathedral, but it was eventually created a Collegiate Church by Elizabeth I in 1560. Its survival was undoubtedly due to its great historical significance as the place of coronation, and the burial place of kings. The Reformation, however, brought a very great change to the interior: the chapels quickly became the ideal receptacles for monuments to relatives of Elizabeth I and members of her court. Both restraint and reticence were abandoned. During the later 16th century, a group of protestant sculptors, refugees from the Netherlands, arrived in England. As aliens, they settled outside the City of London, several in Southwark, on the south side of the Thames: they thus collectively became known as the Southwark School. They brought with them new ideas for monuments, many of which at their most splendid and uninhibited can be seen in the Abbey's eastern chapels, including those to the queen's first cousin, Lord Hunsdon (d 1596), the Countess of Sussex (d 1589) [36], and Lady Fane (d 1618) [46]. The fashion was for colour, portrayal of sons and daughters, and lavish displays of heraldry. This was important in order to establish a respectable and, if possible, ancient lineage for the new Tudor aristocracy.

From the same School of craftsmen, James I commissioned the monuments to his mother, Mary, Queen of Scots, and his cousin, Elizabeth I [38]. These are in the south and north aisles of Henry VII's chapel, and are the last royal monuments in the Abbey. Although recognizably still in the tradition and style of earlier monuments, with plenty of heraldry, it is obvious that there was a change in taste. There is not so much colour, and the effigies are no longer of painted alabaster, but of fine white marble, which contrasts well with the black marble of the architectural framework; the result is much more restrained and dignified. While the face of Mary, Queen of Scots, is only an ideal impression, that of Elizabeth I is undoubtedly a portrait.

The increasing acceptance of less flamboyant memorials during the later years of James I and in the reign of Charles I, was due primarily to an English sculptor, Nicholas Stone, who had worked in the Low Countries. Not only did he avoid colour, but he introduced new forms, such as the seated or standing figure, and he sometimes incorporated decorative design by the architect Inigo Jones. Henry VII's chapel had been exclusively reserved for the royal family, until Charles I allowed the monument to his favourite, George Villiers, Duke of Buckingham [40]. The gilt bronze effigies of the Duke and Duchess, by a Frenchman, Hubert Le Sueur, are undoubtedly influenced by the tomb of Henry VII, as was also the monument to Charles I's cousin, Ludovic Stuart, Duke of Richmond and Lennox (d 1624), also by Le Sueur [45]. Unfortunately, both monuments are far too large for the chapels in which they are confined.

The character of interment and memorialization in the Abbey was, by the mid-17th century, gradually changing and becoming less exclusive. But it seems to have been Oliver Cromwell who was the first to consider the Abbey as the national valhalla. He and several of his followers were buried in the church, but not for long, as Charles II ordered the eviction of their bodies at the Restoration of 1660 and the destruction of any monuments. The only one that appears to have survived this command is that to Colonel Edward Popham in the chapel of St John the Baptist.

From the later 17th century, the Dean and Chapter faced mounting bills for the maintenance of the building, and an admirable source of revenue was found in the fees for both interments and monuments, although the decision to allow these was, and still is, that of the Dean alone. People took advantage of this relaxation, and the walls of the church began to be covered with marble. Unfortunately, the style of the building itself was now regarded as uncouth, barbarous, 'gothic'. As a result, scant regard was paid to the fabric, which was hacked about in outrageous fashion in order to install memorials, particularly in the nave and transepts. Even so, there were only about 150 monuments in the whole of the building by the 1720s; although a few were of considerable size, none was quite so gigantic as that designed by the architect James Gibbs to the Duke of Newcastle in the north transept (1723). Poets' Corner was by now firmly established in the south transept, and in the north choir aisle several musicians were grouped, including Henry Purcell (d 1695)[11], John Blow (d 1708)[12] and William Croft (d 1727), all Abbey organists.

John Dart, who recorded all the monuments as they were during the first years of the 1720s, described them in verse:

> Upon their Backs the ancient Statues lie,
> Devoutly fix'd with Hands up-lifted high,
> Intreating Pray'rs of all the Passers by.
> At length they chang'd the Posture by degrees,
> And placed the Marble Vot'ry on its Knees:
> Then Warriors rough devoutly Heav'n adore,
> And Statesmen kneel, who never kneel'd before:
> Then Ornaments superfluous were known,
> To spoil the native Beauty of the Stone:
> The rich-vein'd Porph'ry we, surpriz'd, behold,
> Vermilion painted, and inlay'd with Gold;
> Where long Inscriptions at such Distance lie,
> Not to be read by the inspecting Eye.
> Next a less pious Posture they provide,
> On Cushions lolling, stretch'd with careless Pride.
> With wringing Hands the little Cherubs moan,
> And Fun'ral Lamps appear to blaze in Stone,
> And Marble Urns with juster Beauty stand,
> And rich Relievo shows the Master's Hand . . .

It is perhaps a relief that Dart wrote when he did, and had not to overtax his descriptive powers on later monuments, for at about this period there arrived in this country, again from the Netherlands, two notable sculptor immigrants, Michael Rysbrack and Peter Scheemakers. At first, Rysbrack was the more successful, obtaining many commissions in the Abbey, notably the two monuments at the east end of the nave, to Sir Isaac Newton (d 1727)[8] and Earl Stanhope (d 1721), both designed by William Kent. But Scheemakers had his revenge, when he was acclaimed by the cognoscenti for his statue of Shakespeare (also designed by Kent)[57] in 1740.

Although the unveiling of these important works was a social occasion for London, none excited more interest than the mid-18th-century rococo creations of a Frenchman, Louis François Roubiliac, who spent his working life in London. There are several of his works in the Abbey: a pyramid toppling on the Day of Judgment and Time vanquishing Death[67], Handel standing transfixed listening to music[59], the figure of Eloquence addressing the viewer of the Duke of Argyll's monument[58], which has the figure of History inscribing his name, but stopping short at 'GR' to indicate that the Dukedom of Greenwich died with him; and the spectacular Nightingale monument[30] on which, from a vault, the skeleton Death hurls his lance. Many of these works had to be hoisted onto window-ledges, as wall space had virtually been exhausted. Criticism of overcrowding began to mount, but this was not the only reason for complaint for, during the 18th and 19th centuries, appreciation of the Abbey as a building began to increase, and voices were raised against the introduction of such an excess of white marble, and what were then considered 'pagan' sculptures [2, 23, 25]. Others were worried about damage caused by sculptors' workmen.

In 1772, a writer to the *Gentleman's Magazine* wrote bitterly about the 'huge quarry of marble, in memory of the late Earl and Countess of Montrath'[28], which had been 'most invidiously placed, as if to eclipse and overshadow ... that masterpiece of Roubiliac's', the Nightingale monument. He complained that the Mountrath monument 'projects three yards ... into the middle of the chapel'. At the same time, he drew attention to the fact that the workmen erecting Joseph Wilton's monument to General Wolfe[31], 'have by their carelessness much damaged and defaced the kneeling figures that support the monumental table of Sir Francis Vere[32]; thus destroying with one hand, while they rear with the other.'

By the 1820s, monuments numbered more than 300, and in order to find space and yet more space (both for monuments and, more importantly, for people), several memorials were either removed entirely, or drastically reduced in size during the 19th century. For example, the Mountrath monument, carved by Joseph Wilton to the design of the architect Sir William Chambers, was cut down in size, thereby losing a key element in its design. Flaxman's Earl of Mansfield [21] was hauled back thus releasing a considerable area for seats, and Admiral Warren [26] lost his background of naval trophies. Two cherubs from Sir Gilbert Lort's monument survive in Little Cloister; Admiral Richard Tyrrell [72] no longer is seen ascending to Heaven, while another monument was removed to make room for the large construction to the memory of Sir Henry Campbell-Bannerman, the Prime Minister who died in 1908. John Keble [62], once part of a standing monument, is now reduced to a bust on a bracket, and is all the better for that. The monuments by Rysbrack to John Gay and Nicholas Rowe were taken up to the triforium in the 1930s when medieval paintings were discovered behind them. As recently as 1960, the huge, weighty and ungainly seated figure of the engineer James Watt, by Sir Francis Chantrey, was removed to the Transport Museum at Clapham. When that closed down, it was hoped that the statue would go to the Railway Museum at York. It was not wanted there, nor by the Victoria and Albert Museum; at length a home was found for it in the crypt of St Paul's Cathedral.

But all this shifting and reduction creates puzzles. In the north nave aisle is a horizontal strip of marble, lettered at an angle, to Elizabeth Carteret (d 1717); the rest of the monument is now at Haynes in Bedfordshire. Originally, this panel of marble represented a shaft of light, descending through clouds. In addition, the palm-trees which overlaid the columns in the north transept on the monument, designed by 'Athenian' Stuart and carved by Scheemakers, to Admiral Watson [18], were removed in 1957, thus reducing a sculptural composition to three isolated figures.

The overcrowding suffered by the Abbey eventually brought a government decision that, so far as possible, those soldiers and sailors killed during the Napoleonic Wars would be commemorated in St Paul's. In consequence the Cathedral contains memorials to later commanders, including those of the last war, as well as to many painters and sculptors, whom the Abbey conspicuously lacks. For the last century, memorials have tended to be busts, while for official monuments to statesmen, over-lifesized standing marble figures were introduced in the north transept [27]. When Gladstone was shown the wording for Disraeli's pedestal there, it is said that he snorted, 'Twice Prime Minister! That's no great distinction.' In an attempt to find, or create space for these national memorials, a Royal Commission at the end of the 19th century sought in vain to decide on whether there should be built a national mausoleum somewhere near to the

Abbey. As a result, in modern times memorials have nearly always been in the form of small slabs let into the floor [52]. In preparation for the 900th anniversary of the consecration of Edward the Confessor's Abbey in 1965, all the monuments were cleaned, and many repainted. After centuries of accumulating grime, the contrast was startling; and, because they could be properly seen for the first time for generations, it came as a revelation.

As there are so many monuments, and several of them are immense, they tend to overwhelm the viewer. The advantage of a book of photographs is that details which otherwise might be overlooked, are singled out. There are Sir Richard Westmacott's fine sculpture of a freed slave [2], or the allegorical women mourning Spencer Perceval [5]. Note also the wrong spelling of Ben Jonson's name on both his grave-marker in the north nave aisle [6], and on his monument by Rysbrack in Poets' Corner [53], or the battering-ram on the rostral column by Francis Bird to Admiral Baker [7]. Among the many portraits, the finest is that of Sir Isaac Newton, but so many others repay study, among them Milton [53], or the sensitive face of John Keble [62], or that of the dramatist, William Congreve [73], based on a painting by Sir Godfrey Kneller, and can that of William Wilberforce [9] really be a caricature, for which it has sometimes been criticized? Lurking on so many of the memorials are animals: there are the heraldic porcupine of the Countess of Sussex [36], a splendid sea-horse by Nollekens [24], and the beaver on John Bacon's monument to an 18th-century Lieutenant-Governor of Quebec [20]. A particular joy among all the lions is the shaggy, miniature one [50] on the neo-classical memorial to the Duchess of Northumberland, designed by Robert Adam. The same architect designed the relief of Major André brought before George Washington as a spy [66] during the American War of Independence, as well as the Red Indians on the monument to Colonel Townshend [65]. Some absurdities become apparent: how do the two little boys support the immense weight of Almeric de Courcy on their shoulders [10], and why is the dying General Wolfe naked, but being attended by two soldiers in full-dress [31]? Costume, particularly of the Elizabethan and Jacobean period, and armour, whether contemporary [32] or Roman [48], can be studied everywhere; Mrs Kendall [33], for instance, is in early-18th century fashion, but, especially during the later 18th century, many people, if they are clothed at all, are in loose classical drapery. Of the nude figures, which are perhaps surprising to find in a church, the most sensitive is probably that of the youth who appears as Death, on the back of Lord Mansfield's pedestal by John Flaxman [21].

But there is so much else to see – a variety of carved lettering [11, 12]; the *graffiti*, among which we find the initials of Izaak Walton [63]; the splendidly carved, disabled H.M.S. *Buckingham* [72]; and among the rococo sculpture of Sir Henry Cheere, sea-shells [14], or the mitre accompanied by oak-leaves, acorns and little cherub-heads [15]. Not to be missed either are the delicate Art Nouveau bronze figures by Sir Alfred Gilbert (the sculptor of Eros in Piccadilly Circus), on the monument to the blind Postmaster-General, Henry Fawcett [75].

Westminster Abbey is most certainly not a museum. Although hundreds of thousands of people come each year especially to see these monuments, it must be remembered that they are in a church – a living church, which has several services every day, hourly prayers, in which people of many nationalities join, and frequent great services of a national character.

JOHN PHYSICK

THE PLATES

FOR
DISCIPLINE ESTABLISHED
FORTRESSES PROTECTED
SETTLEMENTS EXTENDED
FRENCH
AND INDIAN ARMIES
DEFEATED
AND
PEACE CONCLUDED
IN THE CARNATIC

O RARE

BEN JOHNSON

Here lyes
HENRY PVRCELL Esq.
Who left this Life
And is gone to that Blessed Place
Where only his Harmony
can be excceeded
Obijt 21mo die Novembrs
Anno Ætatis suæ 37mo
Annoq^s Domini 1695

He was ~~teacher to~~ his ~~friend~~ ~~Mufici~~
Dᵣ Christopher Gibbons
and Master to the famous Mᵣ H. Purcell
and most of the Eminent Masters in Muſick
He died Octob: yᵉ Jˢᵗ J708 in yᵉ 60ᵗʰ year of his ~~a~~

His own Muſical Compoſitions,
(Eſpecially his Church Muſick)
are a far nobler Monument
to his Memory,
than any other can be raiſd
for Him.

...ed to the Memory of

...AREZ Esq.ʳ One of the Few whose

...er to be meafured by their Actions

...n sixteen to thirty seven years of Age

...and was often surrounded with Dangers

...always approving himself, an able, active,

...out a Lieut.ᵗ on board his Majesties Ship yᵉ CENTURION

...ct of Commodore ANSON in his Expedition to

...Commanding Officer of the said Ship when

...er Moorings at the Isle of TINIAN,

...the NOTTINGHAM a 60 Gun Ship He (then alone)

...RS a French Ship of 64 Guns. In the first

...wing Year, when Admiral ANSON

...dron of French Men of War & India Men,

...e, and in the Second under Admiral HAWKE,

...ce was again

H: Cheere Fecit

... the Remains
... JOHN WARREN, D.D.
... Saint David's, in 1779;
... to the See of Bangor, in 1783.
... Episcopal Stations he filled
for more than twenty Years,
with great Ability and Virtue.
His Charity, Liberality, Candour and Benevolence,
will long be remembered.
His eminent Learning and unwearied Application
rendered him highly serviceable to the Laws,
as well as the Religion of his Country,
towards which he was most sincerely attached:
He was Son of Richard Warren, D.D.
Rector of Cavendish and Archdeacon of Suffolk;
and Brother of Richard Warren, M.D.
celebrated for his Knowledge & successful Practice,
and many Years Physician in Ordinary to His Majesty,
He married Elizabeth Southwell, Daughter of
Henry Southwell, Esq; of Wisbech, Cambridgeshire;
who fully sensible of his many distinguished Virtues,
has offered this grateful Tribute to his Memory,
with the most unfeigned Sincerity and Respect.
He died on the 27th of January, 1800,
in the 72d Year of his Age.

GHEREAH
TAKEN
FEBRVARY XIII

John Bacon, R.A.
Sculptor, 1793.

25

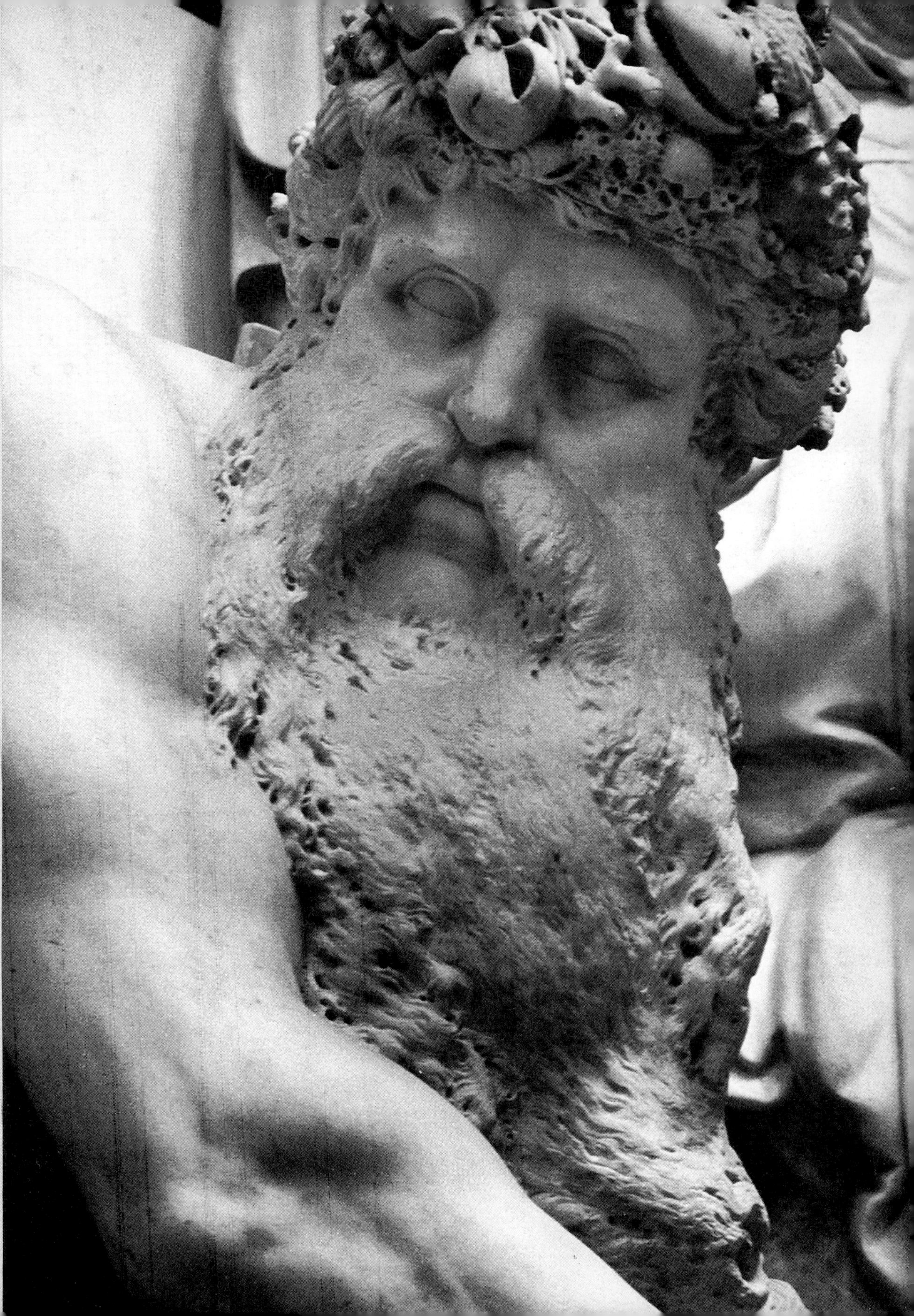

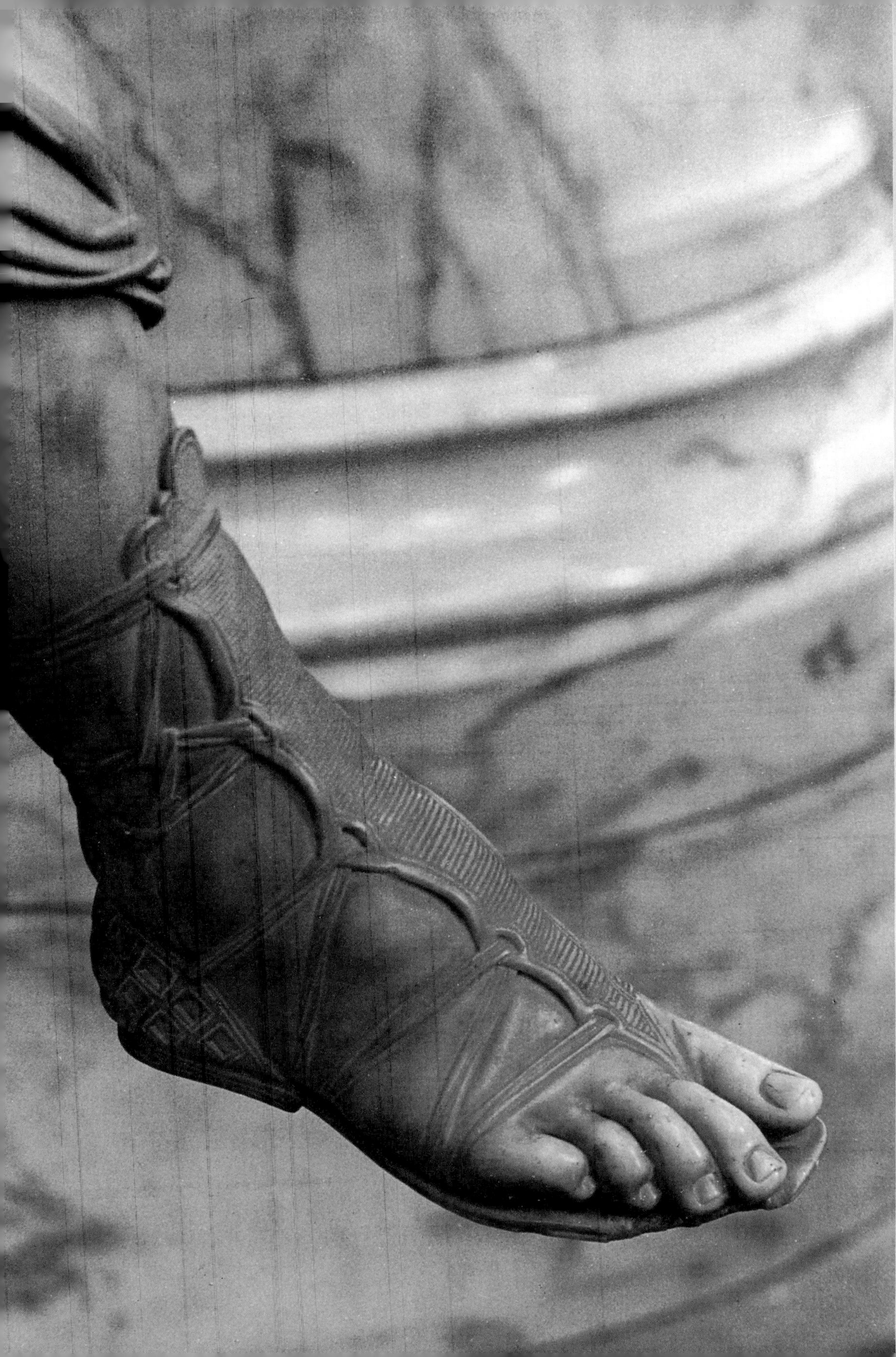

◄ 25

26

ROBERT PEEL.
BORN FEB. 5. 1788 DIED JULY 2. 1850

Here reft the A[...]
JOSEPH GASCOIGNE N[...]
of Mainhead in the Co[...]
Esq.r who died July the 2[...]
    And of Lady ELIZABETH [...]
Daughter and Coheir of WA[...]
Earl Ferrers; who died A[...]
                    aged 27

Their only Son WASHINGTON [...]
NIGHTINGALE Esq.[...] by his Last w[...]
of their virtues [...] to be [...]
order this Mon[...]

30

31 ▶

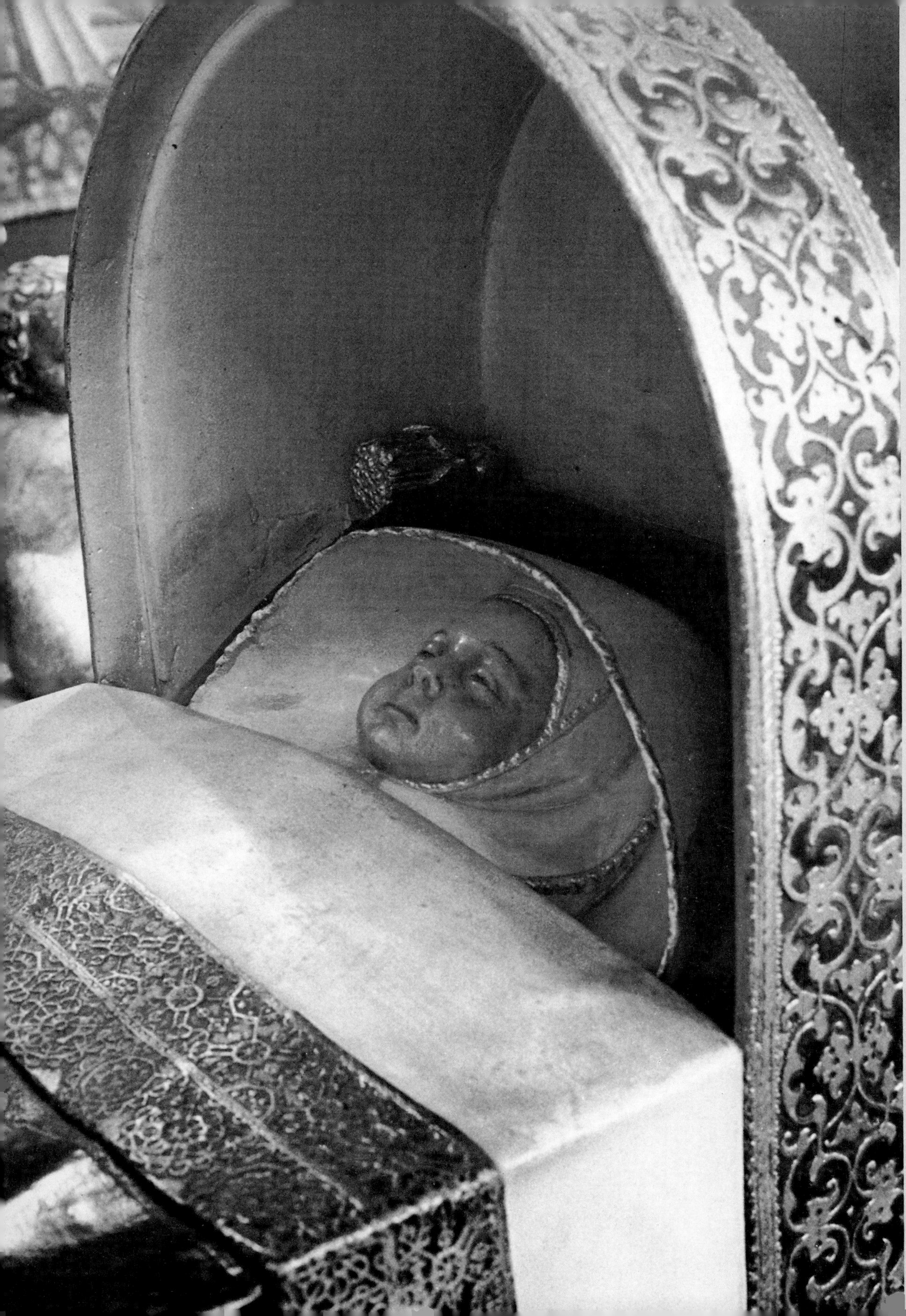

◄ 37
38
39

DEPOSITVM ILLVSTRISSIMI ET EXCELLENTISSIMI PRINCIPIS
LVDOVICI STVARTI ESMEI LEVINIÆ DVCIS FILII, IOANNIS PROPATRVI SERMI
REGIS IACOBI NEPOTIS, RICHMONDIÆ ET LEVINIÆ DVCIS, NOVI CASTELLI
AD TINAM ET DARNLIÆ COMITIS, &C MAGNI SCOTIÆ CAMERARII ET
THALASSIARCHÆ HÆREDITARIÆ SACRI PALATII IACOBI REGIS SENESCHALLI
CVBICVLARIORVMQ PRINCIPALIVM PRIMI, REGI A SANCTIORIBVS CONSILIIS,
SAN = GEORGIANI ORDINIS EQ, SCOTICORVMQ PER GALLIAS
CATAPHRACTORVM PREFECTI,
VIRI EXCELSI AD OMNIA MAGNA ET BONA NATI AD MELIORA DEFVNCTI

49

50 ►

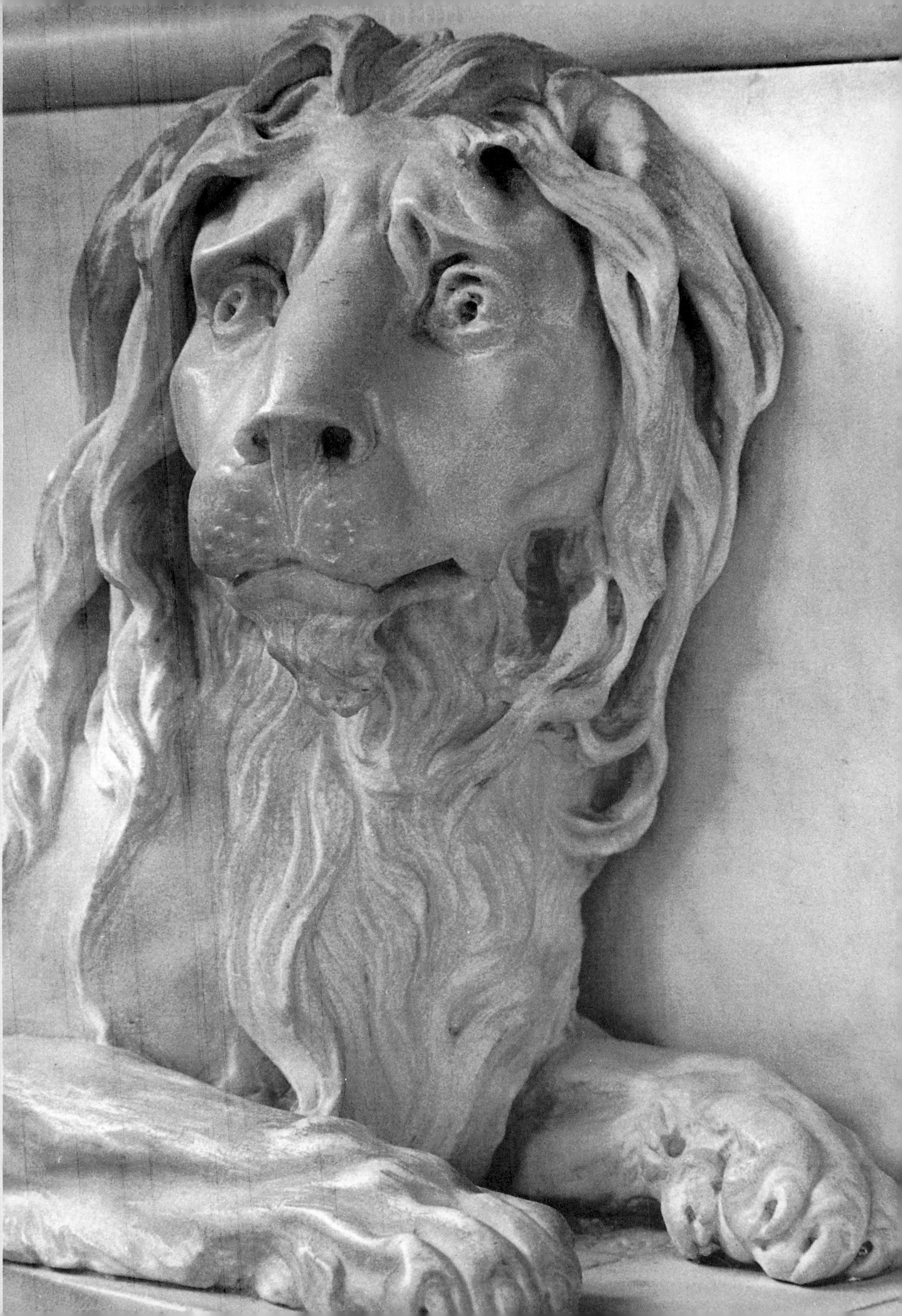

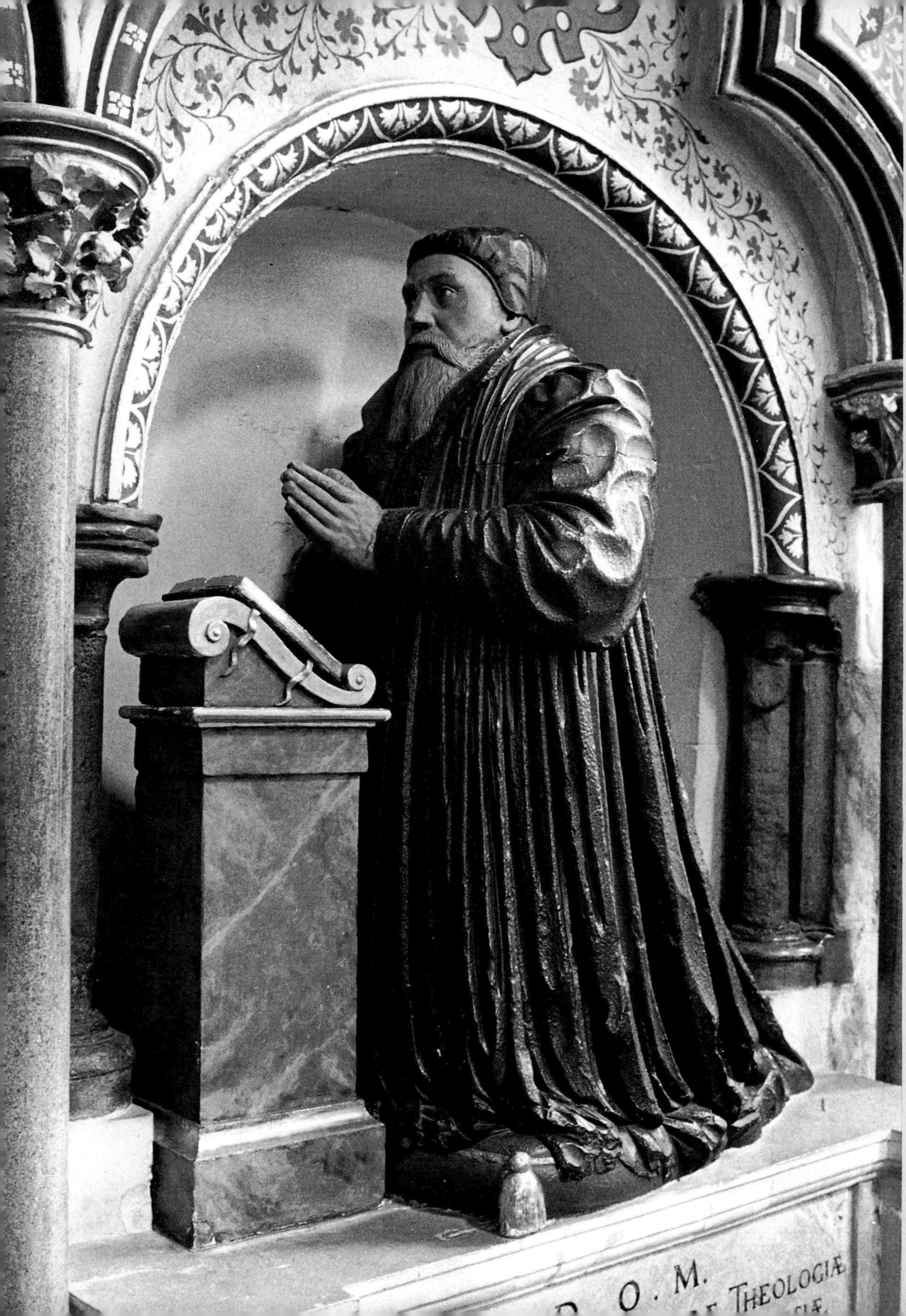

◄ 51

52

GEORGE

HENRY
JAMES
O.M.
Novelist
New York 1843
London 1916

THOMAS
STEARNS
ELIOT

NIS 'TO
CARRO
...Is all our life then...
buried at Guildford

RICHARD ALDINGTON
LAURENCE BINYON
EDMUND BLUNDEN
RUPERT BROOKE
WILFRID GIBSON
ROBERT GRAVES
JULIAN GRENFELL
IVOR GURNEY
DAVID JONES
ROBERT NIC...

Adventurer

EDWARD
LEAR
1812~1888
Painter and Poet
Buried in San Remo

O RARE BEN: IOHNSON

No more the *Græcian* Muſe unrival'd reigns;
To *Britain* let the Nations homage pay;
She felt a HOMER's fire in MILTON's ſtrains,
A PINDAR's rapture in the Lyre of *GRAY.*

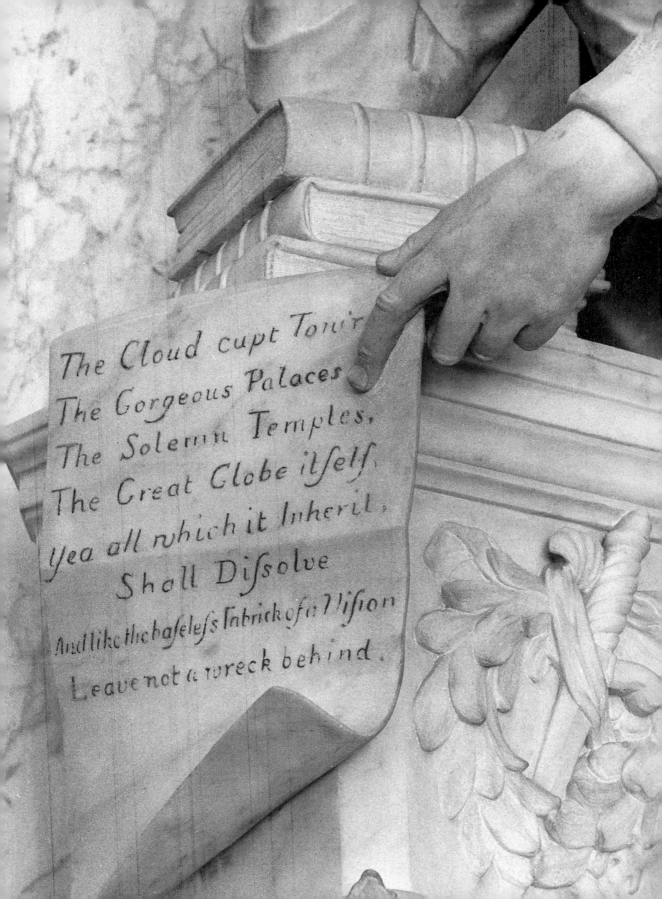

JOHN DUKE OF ARGYLL

GR

Born
October the 10ᵗ
MDCLXXX.
Died
October the 4ᵗʰ
MDCCXLIII.

In Memory of an Honest Man, A
Constant Friend, JOHN the Great DUKE
of ARGYLL and GREENWICH a General
... Orator exceeded by none in the Age
he lived.
& HENRY FIRMER Deviser, by his left, will

GEORGE FREDERICK HANDEL Esq.
born February XXIII. MDCLXXXIV.
died April XIV. MDCCLIX.

L.F.Roubiliac inv.¹ et sc.¹

LICVIT CONS

MEMOR PR

MDCX

IVI

1655

LT CASAVBONV

CHARTAS LEGAT

65

66

To ... ... HARGRAVE Esq.
... ...onel of the Royal English Fuziliers,
... ...d Governor ... ...BRALTAR
... ...ving ... ...ars

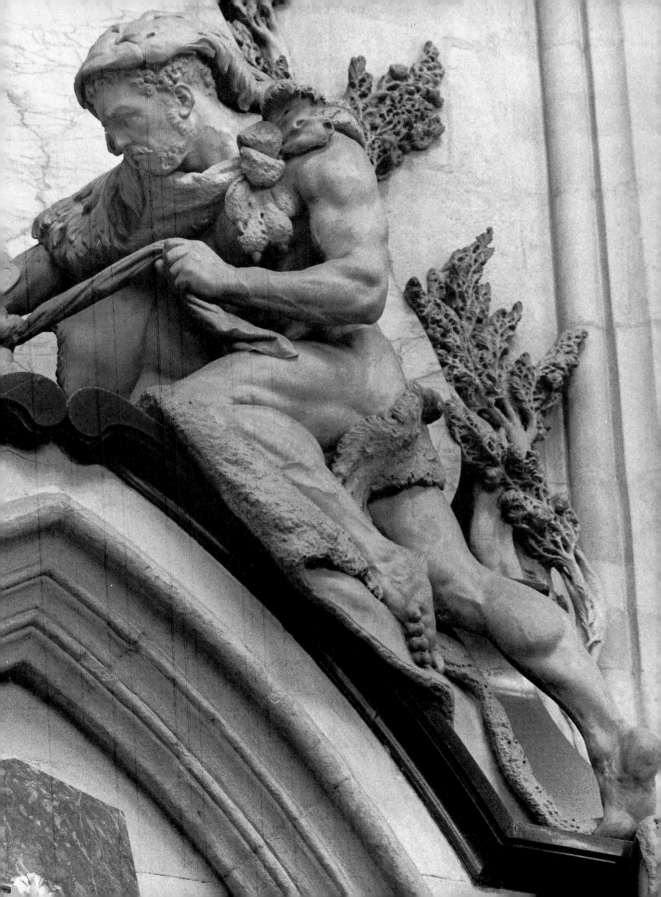

JARY 29TH 1803
RCH 11TH 1863
BEY AT THE PUBLIC COST

TO THE MEMORY
A SOLDIER OF THE EAST
BY DEEDS OF BRAVERY

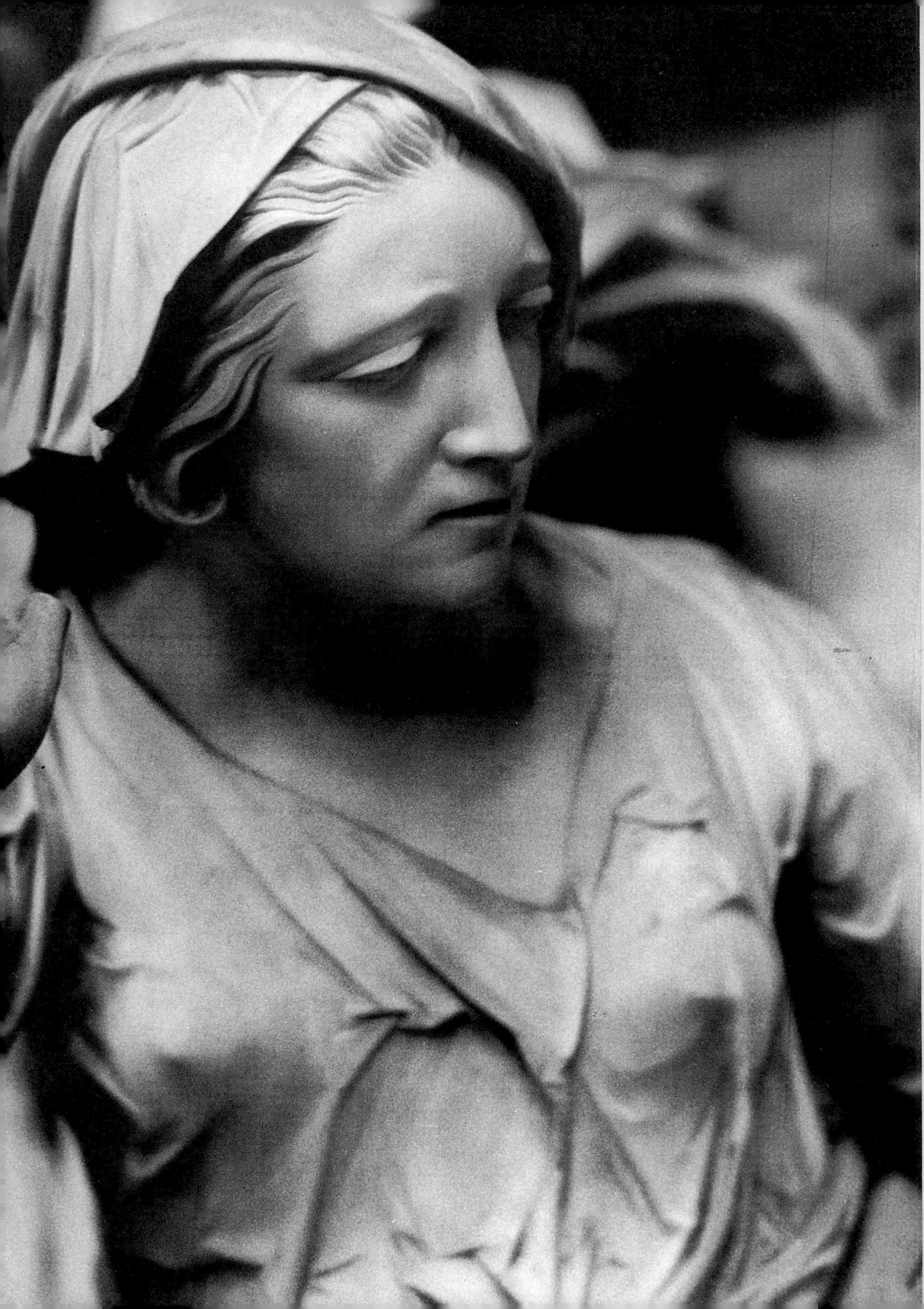

7

BUCKINGHAM

BENEATH THIS STONE RESTS THE BODY
OF A BRITISH WARRIOR
UNKNOWN BY NAME OR RANK
BROUGHT FROM FRANCE TO LIE AMONG
THE MOST ILLUSTRIOUS OF THE LAND
AND BURIED HERE ON ARMISTICE DAY
11 NOV. 1920, IN THE PRESENCE
HIS MAJESTY KING GEOR
HIS MINISTERS OF
THE CHIEFS OF H
AND A VAST CONCOU

THUS ARE COM
MULTITUDE
WAR OF

THE LORD KNOWETH THEM THAT ARE HIS

WE LIVE

X X X

CAPTIONS

Compiled by Jill Waters

Illustrations with the same number show different details of the same monument. More general allegorical figures or animals have not been commented on in the captions. The date after the subject of the monument is that of his death; that after the sculptor is the date of the monument, where this differs. The abbreviation 'des.' is for 'designed'.

1   Lord Holland 1840, Edward Hodges Baily 1845

Henry Fox, third Lord Holland, was an eminent Whig politician who followed his uncle Charles James Fox [2] in his fight against slavery. Whilst travelling abroad in his youth he met both Nelson and Napoleon and he remained an admirer of the latter, opposing the Bill for his detention, also demanding an inquiry into conditions on St Helena. His London residence was Holland House where he and his formidable wife entertained the political and literary world. His monument became known as the 'Prison House of Death'.

2   Charles James Fox 1806, Sir Richard Westmacott 1810

A great Whig politician and lifelong rival of William Pitt the Younger, who died in the same year and is buried nearby. A leading opponent of British Policy in the American War of Independence, Fox died while campaigning for the abolition of the slave trade; he is depicted in the arms of Liberty while Peace and a slave mourn. The figure of Liberty lost her cap during the erection of the scaffolding for the coronation of Queen Victoria.

3   General Stringer Lawrence 1775, William Tyler

Commander of the East India Company forces between 1746 and 1766 and called 'the Father of the Indian Army'. The monument was erected by the Company 'For discipline established, for-

tresses protected, settlements extended, French and Indian armies defeated and peace concluded in the Carnatic' (South-East India).

4   Mrs Mary Beaufoy 1705, Grinling Gibbons

The only reason for her burial in the Abbey appears to be that her parents could afford it. Mrs Beaufoy was the only daughter and heir of Sir Henry Beaufoy of Guyscliffe near Warwick. The monument was erected by her mother who was as anxious to announce on the inscription that 'This monument was made by Mr Grinling Gibbons', as to make her sorrow public.

5   Spencer Perceval 1812, Sir R. Westmacott 1816

Perceval is remembered today as the only British prime minister to have been murdered, rather than for his achievements in office. He was shot by John Bellingham, a crazed bankrupt with a grudge against the authorities. Bellingham's plea of insanity was later set aside by the court and he was hanged. The monument's allegorical figures are a little obscure; seated at Perceval's head is the mourning figure of Power, whilst Truth and Temperance stand at his feet. Backed by a relief of the murder, it was erected by the Prince Regent and Parliament 'to mark the nation's abhorrence of the act by which he fell'.

6   Ben Jonson 1637

'Give me eighteen inches of square ground', Jonson is reputed to have asked as a favour from King Charles I. 'Where?' 'In Westminster Abbey', replied the poet. This account provides

115

an explanation of the story that he was buried standing upright; further evidence came to light in 1849 when Sir Robert Wilson was buried nearby and the clerk in charge 'Saw the two leg bones of Jonson fixed bolt upright in the sand . . . and the skull came rolling down from a position above the leg bones'. The inscribed stone which marked the spot 'was donne at the charge of Jack Young, afterwards knighted, who walking there when the grave was covering, gave the fellow eighteen pence to cutt it', according to John Aubrey in his *Brief Lives*. It was taken up in 1821 when the nave was repaved and later fitted into the north wall. Meanwhile, the original spot has been marked by a lozenge-shaped stone with a copy of the old inscription. It wasn't until 1723, when an anonymous 'person of quality' paid for the monument illustrated in [53], that Ben Jonson finally joined his fellows in Poet's Corner.

7 Vice-Admiral John Baker 1716, Francis Bird

He fought against the French in the War of the Spanish Succession under Sir Cloudesley Shovel and was one of the few whose ships were not lost when Shovel's squadron was wrecked in the Scilly Isles in 1707. Later he pacified the North African corsairs.

8 Isaac Newton 1727, John Michael Rysbrack (des. William Kent) 1731

The mathematician, philosopher and theologian of whom Voltaire wrote, 'If all the geniuses of the universe assembled, he should lead the band'. Newton is chiefly remembered for his formulation of the laws of gravity. Wordsworth [61] wrote some memorable lines about another statue of him (by Roubiliac in Trinity College Chapel, Cambridge): 'The marble index of a mind for ever/Voyaging through strange seas of Thought, alone.' The spot selected for his monument was one of the most conspicuous in the Abbey and had previously been refused to a number of noblemen who had applied for it. From this time, the more sacred recesses of the Abbey were considered closed to memorials, which instead took advantage of the greater publicity of the previously neglected open spaces around the nave and in the transepts. His monument elaborately records in allegorical fashion some of his achievements and is accompanied by a wordy Latin inscription against which Dr Johnson protested vigorously. The diagram brandished by the putto is part of a proof concerning elliptic orbits from Newton's book *De Motu Corporum in Gyrum*. The gothic screen, which obscures the upper part, is a nineteenth-century intrusion.

9 William Wilberforce 1833, Samuel Joseph 1838

'His name will forever be specially identified with those exertions, which by the blessing of God, removed from England the guilt of the African slave trade and prepared the way for the abolition of slavery in every colony of the Empire' – so runs the inscription. The Act of Emancipation was passed twelve months after his death. A special petition was made to the Dean for a grave in the Abbey and his funeral procession was attended by both Houses of Parliament. Some doubt has been cast on the actual likeness of Joseph's sculpture, which is perhaps more of a caricature than a portrait.

10 Almeric de Courcy, Lord Kinsale 1720, sculptor unknown

A staunch supporter of James II. The inscription states that he inherited the privilege granted to John de Courcy in the reign of King John, of remaining covered before the King. It is said that Lord Kinsale once asserted this hereditary right by wearing his hat in the presence of King William III. The back of his (hatless) bewigged head can be seen behind Wilberforce in [9].

11 Henry Purcell 1695, sculptor unknown

Purcell's father was music copyist at Westminster Abbey and at the age of six young Henry became a chorister, thus beginning his musical training and a long association with the Abbey. He composed both religious and dramatic works, gaining widespread acclaim particularly for his 'work of genius,' the opera *Dido and Aeneas*, written when he was only twenty-two. In the same year he became organist at the Abbey and on his death, only fifteen years later, he was buried close to where the organ stood. He is reputed to have died after catching cold because his wife locked him out of the house as a punishment for coming home late. The tablet was erected by his patroness Lady Elizabeth Howard, the wife of Dryden, who is said to have composed the epitaph.

12 Dr John Blow 1708, sculptor unknown

Choirmaster and organist at Westminster Abbey, he presided over the Chapel Royal for thirty-five years. Although he composed a large quantity of religious music, little was published and his talents were outshone by those of his pupil, Purcell. Recognising this he resigned his post of organist in 1680 in favor of the younger man. The celebrated 'Gloria' from his 'Jubilate in C major' is engraved upon his monument.

13 Dame Mary James d. 1677, sculptor unknown

Daughter of Sir Robert Killigrew the courtier, MP and amateur pharmacist; sister of William, Henry, and Thomas Killigrew, all courtiers and dramatists.

14 Captain Philip de Saumarez 1747, Sir Henry Cheere

Fought for his country from his sixteenth to his thirty-seventh year, eventually being killed by what was probably the last shot fired in the action off Cape Finisterre against the French. The base of his monument is decorated with some carefully sculpted sea-shells which are all indigenous to the Channel Isles from which he came.

15 Bishop Hugh Boulter 1742, Cheere

Bishop of Bristol and then of Armagh in 1723; his extensive works of charity earned him the gratitude of the Irish people. But as Lord Justice of Ireland he supported many repressive measures curtailing the freedom of Roman Catholics, excluding them from holding office or pursuing the legal profession.

16 Brigadier-General Richard Kane 1736, Rysbrack

Joined the 18th Irish Foot in 1689 and served in Ireland and Flanders. He was wounded in Lord Cutts' desperate assault on the castle of Namur, 1695. He was later made Governor of Gibraltar and Minorca and was buried at St Philip's castle in Minorca.

17 Bishop John Warren 1800, Sir R. Westmacott

Warren became Bishop of Bangor in 1783 having previously been Bishop of St David's. He married Elizabeth Southwell of Cambridgeshire who brought him a great fortune; see [23].

18 Read-Admiral Charles Watson 1757, Peter Scheemakers (des. James 'Athenian' Stuart)

He earned his fame in India, in joint operations with Robert Clive, capturing Gheriah, a pirate stronghold south of Bombay, and then avenging the 'Black Hole of Calcutta'.

19 Lieutenant-General Joshua Guest 1747, Sir Robert Taylor 1752

He started life as an inn servant and always remembered his humble origins. He would send a plate from his own table to the sentry at the door saying, 'I remember when I stood sentinel I often had abundant cause to envy those at dinner inside.' He fought with distinction under King William in Ireland and Flanders and also in the Cadiz expedition of 1702. Despite his rumoured Jacobite sympathies, he successfully held Edinburgh Castle against the rebels in 1745; he did not, as is implied by his monument's inscription, die during the siege but in London two years later.

20 Brigadier-General Adrian Hope 1789, John Bacon the Elder, 1793

One of the first British Governors of Quebec, until 1763 in the Province of New France. The beaver is now one of Canada's national emblems.

21   Earl of Mansfield 1793, John Flaxman 1795

Born William Murray, fourth son of Viscount Stormont, at Oxford he began a lifelong rivalry with William Pitt [25] by defeating him in a Latin competition. He continued his studies in law and his eloquence soon won him the position of Solicitor-General; he was later to be Lord Chief Justice. His most famous judgments show both liberal and repressive characteristics. He was responsible for fining and imprisoning the famous radical politician John Wilkes, who accused Mansfield of subverting the laws of the land and refusing free speech. But when a negro in chains was brought before him, he judged the case on the simple grounds that slavery was 'so odious' that nothing could 'be suffered to support it but positive law,' and released the slave. Many of his judgments created legal precedents and he was renowned as a model of impartiality, even in conducting the trials after the Gordon Riots in which his own house was sacked and burned. A large sum of money was left by a friend to pay for the erection of the Abbey monument. Kenwood on the edge of Hampstead Heath was his country home.

22   Sir Eyre Coote 1783, Thomas Banks

Joined the army at an early age and was with the first British regiment to be sent to India in 1754. By 1777 he had become Commander-in-Chief of the East India Company forces on whose behalf he expelled the French from the coast of Coromandel (S.E. India). After defeating Hyder Ali, the ruler of Mysore and ally of the French, he was returning to Madras and recovering from ill-health when the ship on which he was sailing was chased by a French cruiser. It is said that he was so upset by this incident that he suffered a relapse and died a few days later.

23   Mrs Warren 1816, Sir R. Westmacott

Wife of Bishop John Warren [17], she spent much of her fortune charitably and her benevolence is typified by the figure of the beggar-girl nursing a baby, 'The Distressed Mother'.

24   Captains Lord Robert Manners, Bayne and Blair 1782, Joseph Nollekens

All of the 'Three Captains' were killed in action against the French at the Battle of Dominica in the West Indies. Manners was only twenty-four when he died, having been promoted at an early age after the exertion of influence by his father, the famous Marquis of Granby (seen today on a hundred pub signs); Lord Sandwich had written to Vice-Admiral Rodney, 'there is another young man of fashion now in your squadron concerning whom I am tormented to death ... therefore if you could continue to give him rank, you will infinitely oblige me.' Bayne and Blair, had been promoted without aristocratic interference after service in North America and in Europe against the French. The monument was erected to all three by the King and Parliament.

25   William Pitt The Elder, Earl of Chatham 1778, John Bacon the Elder 1779

Minister who oversaw the defeat of the French in the Seven Years' War. The City of London wished to bury him at St Pauls within the commercial city whose trading empire he had done so much to protect and extend, but Parliament had already decided on Westminster in order that he 'be brought near to the dust of kings'. The erection of his monument in the north transept began what was to become a Statesman's Corner, yet as Macaulay wrote, 'among the eminent men whose bones lie near his, scarcely one has left a more stainless, and none a more splendid name.' The enthusiastic inscription on the monument was written by the sculptor and approved by George III with the words, 'Now, Bacon, mind you do not turn author, stick to your chisel.'

26   Vice-Admiral Sir Peter Warren 1752, Louis François Roubiliac 1753

Having joined the navy as a volunteer seaman in 1717, he was promoted steadily, serving largely in the West Indies and off the coast of North America. He commanded the attack which captured Louisburg, controlling the entrance to the St Lawrence river in Canada, from the French in 1745. Warren was subsequently appointed vice-admiral but due to ill-health he returned to London with his riches in 1747 and became Member of Parliament for Westminster until his death five years later. Warren is depicted with his face pitted with small-pox, whilst the equally realistic figure of Hercules who stands over him, is reputed to have been modelled on a prize-fighter. The figure of the seated woman with a prow of a ship crowning her head represents Navigation whose melancholy and admiring gaze is directed at the admiral. She is resting on a cornucopia which perhaps echoes the rich booty that Warren captured. The tip protrudes from her right side whilst the full end of the horn is to her left. Roubiliac's monument has been described both as 'singularly tasteless' and 'superb'; it was so truncated in the nineteenth century that it cannot be fairly judged today.

27 Prime Ministers and Cannings

By the 1830s, there was no wall space left, so free-standing figures, mostly of prime ministers, started to occupy floor space, particularly in the north transept. In receding order: Peel by John Gibson, Gladstone by Sir Thomas Brock, Disraeli by Sir Edgar Boehm, Sir John Malcolm the Indian administrator and diplomatist, Earl Canning, Governor-General of India during the Mutiny where he earned the name 'Clemency Canning', George Canning the Prime Minister by Sir Francis Chantrey.

28 The Earl and Countess of Mountrath 1771, Joseph Wilton (des. Sir William Chambers)

Coote was the name of this family, whose fortunes were made as military commanders in Ireland between 1600 and 1660. Sir Eyre Coote [22] was a collateral relation. Before being reduced in size in the last century, the monument showed Lord Mountrath seated in Heaven, awaiting the arrival of his widow, an empty chair at his side. It is towards this that the angel is giving Lady Mountrath a helping hand.

29 Captain Edward Cooke 1779, John Bacon the Younger 1799

A naval captain for the East India Company, which erected the monument. Cooke died of wounds received in a dramatically successful frigate action in which his ship the *Sybille* captured the French frigate *Forte* in the Bay of Bengal.

30 Joseph and Lady Elizabeth Nightingale 1731, Roubiliac 1761

Daughter of Washington, Earl Ferrers, she died at the age of twenty-seven as the result of a premature childbirth brought on by a fright caused by a sudden flash of lightning. Roubiliac depicts her husband (whose ashes the tomb also contains – he outlived her by twenty years) vainly trying to ward off the spectre of Death from his bride. Edmund Burke found the scene 'natural and affecting', but thought that an extinguished torch would have been more suitable for Death to brandish than a dart. For John Wesley it was 'one tomb which showed common sense . . . Here indeed the marble seems to speak'. A Westminster legend corroborates this: a robber was so startled by the vision of Death in the moonlight that he fled, leaving behind a crowbar preserved to this day. The date of death on the monument, 1734, is incorrect.

31 General Wolfe 1759, Wilton 1773

Born into a military family, Wolfe entered the army when he was 16, serving in Flanders and then later with General Wade in Scotland. He shared in the final victory at Culloden under the Duke of Cumberland. His most significant achievement was the capture of Quebec which led to the defeat of the French and the establishment of British rule in Canada. The huge monument, which Pitt had suggested should be erected, depicts Wolfe's death in the moment of victory. The story goes that the night before he repeated nearly the whole of Gray's [54] 'Elegy', 'adding, as he concluded, that he would prefer being the author of that poem to the glory of beating the French tomorrow.'

32 Sir Francis Vere 1609, Maximilian Colt

Having become eligible for the list of 'valiant young gentlemen' competent to command a company in 1586, he embarked on a successful military and diplomatic career which culminated in commanding the British forces in the Netherlands. His wife erected the monument on which the effigy is shown without armour signifying that he died in bed rather than in battle. The photograph is of one of the supporters, not the effigy itself.

33 Mary Kendall 1710, sculptor unknown

All that is known about Mary Kendall is her wish to be buried alongside Lady Catherine Jones. The inscription has the pleasing lines: 'She had great virtues, and as great a desire of concealing them; was of a severe life but of an easy conversation.'

34 Rear-Admiral Charles Holmes 1761, Wilton

Most of his naval service was in the West Indies, taking part in the constant skirmishes against the Spanish. In 1748 following an action off Havana, Rear-Admiral Knowles complained that a number of captains, particularly Holmes, had been disobedient and neglected orders. In the ensuing courts-martial Holmes was the only one to be cleared and indeed commended for his conduct. He subsequently sat as a member of the court-martial of Admiral Byng in 1756. Holmes served under Admiral Saunders as third-in-command of the fleet at the capture of Quebec in 1759; he was then promoted and spent the last eighteen months of his life as commander-in-chief of the fleet in Jamaica where he died.

35 William Pulteney, Earl of Bath 1764, Wilton

Whig politician who conducted a long feud against Sir Robert Walpole which, although based on a difference of opinion on how to solve the national debt, also owed much to personal animosity. Together with other rebel Whigs he formed a group known as the 'Patriots' and had much popular support. However, he eventually succumbed to a peerage in 1742 and lost much political face by so doing. At his funeral there was such a press of spectators that some damage was done to the tomb of Edward I.

36 Frances Sidney, Countess of Sussex 1589, attrib. R. Stevens

The aunt of the poet Sir Philip Sidney and wife of Thomas Radcliffe, Earl of Sussex, known to all readers of Sir Walter Scott's *Kenilworth* as the rival of Leicester. Part of the large fortune she left was to be used to pay for a preacher to read, in her name, two divinity lectures in the Abbey 'every week for ever'. The practice does not still continue but Sidney Sussex College in Cambridge, which the rest of her estate was used to found, does. The porcupines so prominent on her tomb are the Sidney heraldic crest.

37 Princess Sophia 1600, Maximilian Colt

Second daughter of James I, she died within a few days of her birth. She is buried alongside her elder sister, Mary, who died six months later aged $2\frac{1}{2}$ years. The sculptor interrupted his work on the tomb of Elizabeth (which is situated opposite) to make the monuments for the two princesses.

38 Elizabeth I 1603, Colt and de Critz 1606

Known variously as the Virgin Queen and Gloriana, the inscription written by her minister Cecil describes her as 'The Mother of this her Country, Nurse of Religion and Learning'; whilst the lavish tomb was ordered with the words, 'Rather than fail in payment for Queen Elizabeth's tomb neither the Exchequer or London shall have a penny left'. The figure is not original but a replacement from 1760 although the mask is original and was taken from a cast. Her head was crowned and she wore a gilded lead collar of the Garter, but the crown disappeared and the collar was stolen later in the 1820s when the iron rails were removed. A collar and rails were made a few years ago and the crown was replaced in 1985, but stolen again. Elizabeth's death marked the end of the Tudor line and her funeral was not attended by relatives, the closest being Arabella Stuart who refused to take her place as chief mourner because of Elizabeth's harsh treatment of her.

39 Richard II 1400

At the age of ten, Richard was crowned King in Westminster; the order of service used on that occasion was preserved in the *Liber Regalis* and has been followed in every coronation since. The occasion marked the beginning of Richard's long affection for the Abbey and reverence for its saint, Edward the Confessor, his favorite oath being 'by St Edward'. His impulsive nature showed itself in an ugly scene at the Abbey when he struck the Earl of Arundel in anger at his failure to arrive on time for the funeral of his beloved Queen Anne (they had also been married in the Abbey); the service was suspended whilst rites were performed to purify the Abbey after this sacrilegious act. Richard ordered a magnificent tomb for his wife with his own effigy placed alongside her, clasping hands; this record of their love was partially destroyed when Puritan soldiers, stabling their horses in the Abbey, broke off the arms and mutilated Anne's head-dress. After his cousin Henry of Lancaster had manoeuvred Richard into resigning his throne, the ex-King was imprisoned and died at Pontefract. It wasn't until the accession of Henry V that his body was transferred to the Abbey in 1413 to join that of his first wife.

40 George Villiers, Duke of Buckingham 1628, Hubert le Sueur

The hated favorite of James I and subsequently of his son Charles I, whom he addressed as 'Baby Charles'. Loathed by the Commons because of his inordinate influence, Buckingham could do no wrong in the eyes of the two monarchs. He conducted a disastrous foreign policy, leading to a war which caused his attempt to pawn the crown jewels in order to raise money. Buckingham was stabbed to death by a discharged soldier who believed he was acting for God in ridding the country of an evil man. Charles I created a precedent by allowing Buckingham to be buried in the Royal Chapel of Henry VII, together with his wife and three of their sons; but due to popular hostility, the ceremony had to take place privately at night. The monument raised by his widow has been described as 'pretentious and inartistic', but is redeemed by the charming group of the Villiers children placed above their parents.

41 Thomas Bromley 1587, sculptor unknown

Succeeded Sir Nicholas Bacon as Lord Chancellor to Queen Elizabeth in 1579. His dedicated frankness won her favour and respect and he was entrusted with the prosecution of the Catholic conspirator Babington, after whose execution he presided over the trial of Mary Queen of Scots. It was with reluctance that Bromley prepared the execution warrant, but he persuaded the vacillating Elizabeth to sign it in the belief that it would ensure the safety of her crown and person. However, following Mary's execution, the strain proved too much for his constitution and he became ill and died a few months later. His fine marble monument with alabaster effigies was put up by his eldest son; beneath the figure of Bromley kneel his eight children one of whom married Cromwell's uncle and was thus connected with another 'regicide'.

42 First Duke of Buckingham and Normanby 1721, Scheemakers and Laurent Delvaux (des. Denis Plumière)

John Sheffield, Third Earl of Mulgrave, fought at sea in the Dutch Wars and commanded the expedition to relieve Tangier in 1680. In high favour with James II, he quietly submitted to William and Mary, becoming a leading Tory. In 1703 he was made a duke and built Buckingham House (now Buckingham Palace). He was a patron of Dryden and friend of Pope. His third wife, Catharine Sedley, portrayed here, was an illegitimate daughter of James II.

43 Eleanor of Castile 1291, William Torrell

'A princess of great beauty and discretion' who faithfully accompanied her husband King

Edward I on his campaigns – including the 1270 Crusade, when legend has it that she saved his life by sucking the poison from a wound. Twelve crosses commemorated the halting-places of her funeral cortege from Lincoln to burial in the Abbey. Her entrails were buried in Lincoln, her heart in Blackfriars and her body in the Abbey.

44 Henry VII 1509, Pietro Torrigiano, 1518

Henry Tudor won the throne of England at the battle of Bosworth where Richard III was killed. He then united the warring houses of York and Lancaster by marrying Edward IV's daughter, Princess Elizabeth of York, thus bringing an end to the Wars of the Roses. He ruled thriftily and with diplomatic skill, but his parsimony did not extend to the magnificent edifices he erected: the Palace of Richmond, the Chapel of King's College Cambridge and the Chapel at Westminster where his tomb lies. Originally commissioned as a shrine for Henry VI, his predecessor's body was never transferred there. The Lancastrian rose and the Tudor portcullis dominate as they do in King's College Chapel. The greyhound (also present in King's College Chapel) is the York symbol commemorating his wife and comes from the Neville family. The Dragon of Wales indicates the origins of his own family.

45 Ludovic Stuart, Duke of Richmond and Lennox 1624, Le Sueur

A cousin of James Stuart of Scotland, at his birth he became for a time next in line to the throne of Scotland and was sent for by the King and received into his special favour. At the age of fifteen he was appointed president of the council in James's absence. On the accession of James to the English throne he moved south. The huge bronze monument erected by his third wife, Frances Howard, consists of a canopy surmounted by Fame blowing a trumpet and supported by the bronze figures of Faith, Hope, Prudence and Charity. It is Prudence that is illustrated, identifiable by the snake ('Be ye wise as Serpents' – St Matthew's Gospel) and the mirror – the wise see themselves as they really are.

46 Sir George and Lady Elizabeth Fane 1618, sculptor unknown

She was the daughter of the first Baron Spencer. He might have been the brother of Sir Francis Fane who became the first Earl of Westmorland.

47 Elizabeth Russell 1601, sculptor unknown

Daughter of Lord John Russell, she was born within the precincts of the Abbey as her mother had been given permission by the Dean to take refuge there from the plague. She became a maid of honour to her godmother Queen Elizabeth, and for a short time incurred the wrath of her mistress by walking with a friend unchaperoned through the private galleries of Whitehall 'to see the lords and gentlemen play at ballon'. The two girls were soon recalled to court but Elizabeth died of consumption shortly afterwards. Her statue shows her seated, asleep on a basket of osiers, and was the first in the Abbey not to show the figure recumbent upon a tomb. The finger pointing to a skull, an emblem of the Russell family, gave rise to the vulgar error that she died from the prick of a needle, further embellished by the claim that this was a punishment for working on a Sunday.

48 Francis Holles 1622, Nicholas Stone

Younger son of John Holles, first Earl of Clare, the eighteen-year-old Francis fought under his uncle Sir George Holles in the Netherlands but died during the voyage home. The pedestal of the monument was copied from that on which sits Elizabeth Russell in a similar attitude nearby [47]. The Earl of Clare erected the monuments to his son and brother [next to 29 and 32], and the sculptor made a radical departure in cladding both in Roman armour.

49 John of Eltham 1336

The younger son of Edward II, he was made Earl of Cornwall by his brother, Edward III who showed his confidence in the sixteen-year-old John by appointing him Regent on three occasions when the King was obliged to be in

France and Scotland. In his twentieth year, his last, he was entrusted with sole command of Scotland and died at Perth. His body was brought to the Abbey a year later to be laid 'amongst the royals'; the alabaster figure on the tomb remains intact although the canopy was destroyed by the crowd at the funeral of the Duchess of Northumberland in 1776.

50   Duchess of Northumberland 1776, by Nicholas Read (des. Robert Adam)

Born Elizabeth Percy, she was the sole heiress of the first Duke of Northumberland. She also inherited the Seymour family's right to be buried in the Chapel of St Nicholas as her grandmother had married into that family. The Duchess was a generous patron of literature and also known for her charitable works. Although she had expressed the wish that her funeral be as private as her rank 'would admit' it was dominated by a chaotic mob and had to be suspended for some hours until the confusion subsided.

51   Dean Gabriel Goodman 1601

Appointed Dean of the Abbey in 1561. Although nominated many times, he never became a bishop: Archbishop Parker thought him 'too severe', an impression not dispelled by his monument. Goodman presided for forty years at the Abbey and made many improvements including the creation of a garden, the appointment of a keeper for the monuments and the foundation of a hospital for the students of Westminster School.

52   Floor slabs in Poets' Corner

Edward Lear is the latest addition, only put there during the summer of 1988, to mark the centenary of his death.

53   Ben Jonson 1637, Rysbrack (des. James Gibbs) 1723

See [6].

54   Thomas Gray 1771, John Bacon the Elder 1778

Although he left Cambridge without a degree, he remained in close contact with his Etonian friend Horace Walpole who was a contemporary at university and it was Walpole who encouraged him to publish his poetry, the first being his 'Ode on a distant prospect of Eton College'. Gray became acclaimed as a poet and was offered the post of Poet Laureate on Colley Cibber's death, but he declined. He is buried at Stoke Poges which had inspired his 'Elegy in a Country Churchyard'.

55   John Milton 1674, Rysbrack 1737

Milton is remembered today chiefly for his great poetry, *Lycidas, Paradise Lost,* and *Samson Agonistes,* but he was politically active and worked for Cromwell's government writing pamphlets, including his 'Tenure of Kings and Magistrates' arguing for the right of people to judge their rulers. This was the reason for the delay in erecting a monument to him in Poets' Corner. The Whig politician William Benson put up the monument together with an inscription that referred largely to himself, for which both Johnson and Pope took him to task. The poet was buried at St Giles, Cripplegate.

56   Matthew Prior 1721, Rysbrack (des. Gibbs)

Discovered by Lord Dorset reading Horace while working in his uncle's wine shop, Prior became Dorset's protégé. He paid for him to resume his studies at Westminster School from where he won a scholarship to Cambridge. A diplomatic career was crowned by his negotiation of the Treaty of Utrecht ending Marlborough's wars in 1713, known as Mat's peace. The bust on the monument, by the French sculptor Coysevox, was a present from Louis XIV to Prior in about 1700. As a poet, he is remembered for his brilliant occasional pieces and epigrams, an example of which are his lines 'For My Own Monument' beginning:

As Doctors give physic by way of prevention,
Mat, alive and in health, of his tombstone took care;
For delays are unsafe, and his pious intention
May haply be never fulfilled by his heir.

Then take Mat's word for it, the sculptor is
    paid;
That the figure is fine, pray believe your own
    eye;
Yet credit but lightly what more may be said,
For we flatter ourselves, and teach marble to
    lie.

57   William Shakespeare 1616, Scheemakers (des. William Kent) 1740

The monument, which made the sculptor's
name, was paid for by public subscription. The
lines inscribed on the scroll are Prospero's from
The Tempest, generally thought to be Shakespeare's last play. They are slightly out of order.

58   Duke of Argyll 1743, Roubiliac 1749

Distinguished by his bravery under the Duke
of Marlborough, Argyll was less successful as
commander in the 1711 Spanish campaign and
in controlling the first Jacobite rising against
George I in 1715. His career as a statesman is
represented in Roubiliac's allegorical figures of
Eloquence with her hand outstretched on one
side and the helmeted Minerva on the other.
Above, History is recording the second half of
the Duke's title, Greenwich, whilst the volumes
of Demosthenes and Caesar's *Commentaries*
which lie at the foot of Eloquence commemorate
the union of the oratorical and military in him.
His Whig principles are recalled in the sculpture
of The Temple of Liberty and a cherub holding
up the Magna Charta. The monument was
received with rapture by the London public;
Walpole's reaction was typical: 'Mr F. L. Rubil-
liac has shown the greatness of his Genius in his
invention, design and execution in every part
equal, if not superior to any others; this Monument now outshines for nobleness and skill all
those before done, by the best sculptors, this fifty
years past.'

59   George Frederick Handel 1759, Roubiliac 1761

Born in Germany he came to England in 1710
and although returning to Germany for long
visits he spent most of the rest of his life in
London, becoming naturalised in 1726. After
George I's accession he became a favourite court
composer. For George II's coronation he composed the famous 'Zadok the Priest' used ever
since at coronations; whilst for the burial of his
close friend and patron Queen Caroline he wrote
the beautiful 'The ways of Zion do mourn'. In
1753 he became almost totally blind, but continued to dictate compositions to an amanuensis.
The piece of music on the monument is 'I know
that my redeemer Liveth', the most famous aria
from his oratorio *The Messiah*. The face of Roubiliac's statue is from a cast taken after death;
but it is said that the sculptor, dissatisfied with
the shape of the ears, lopped them off and
replaced them with some others from a bust he
had to hand in his studio.

60   John Grabe 1711, Francis Bird

A Prussian by birth, he began to question the
validity of the orders of the Lutheran church, so
came to England because of this religious unease
and continued his theological studies in Oxford.
Granted a royal stipend, he was made chaplain
of Christ Church in 1700. He published new
Latin editions of a number of religious works.
His patron Robert Harley erected this monument
to him.

61   William Wordsworth 1850, Frederick Thrupp

The poet of Nature and childhood, renowned for
his association with the Lake District where he
was born and spent most of his later life, eventually to be buried at Grasmere. His great life work
was his epic *The Prelude* for which he took as a
subject 'the growth of a poet's mind', that is to
say, himself.

62   John Keble 1866, Thomas Woolner

Churchman and scholar who together with
Newman and Pusey took a leading part in the
High-Church or Oxford Movement starting in
1832. His devotional poems *The Christian Year*
were an enormous success with over a hundred
editions published by the time he died. After his
death it was decided to establish a fund to found

an Oxford College where an education in strict fidelity to the Church would be provided. Keble College was opened in 1869.

63   Isaac Casaubon 1614, Nicholas Stone

French Protestant scholar who, like John Grabe [60] found religious sanctuary in England, following the death of his French patron Henry IV. His wife, by whom he had twenty children, was buried with him near St Benedict's Chapel. Isaac Walton, who was a friend of Casaubon's son, has the distinction of being the earliest known author of Abbey graffiti: his initials are scratched on the tomb with the date 1658.

64   David Garrick 1779, Henry Webber 1797

Born in Lichfield and taught by Dr Johnson, Garrick came to London at the age of 20 in order to set up a wine company. However, after participating in some amateur productions, the young Garrick took London by storm with his famous performances as Richard III in 1741. For the next thirty-eight years he dominated the English stage and restored productions of Shakespeare to something resembling the original performances. He died only three years after he had retired from the stage; the funeral was a grand and public affair such as had never been held for an actor. Three lords and a duke were among the pall bearers, whilst Dr Johnson declared that the death of his former pupil had 'impoverished the public stock of harmless pleasure.' Garrick is flanked by the Muses of Comedy and Tragedy.

65   Lieutenant-Colonel Roger Townshend 1759, Thomas and Benjamin Carter and John Eckstein (des. Adam)

Killed by a cannon-ball at the age of 28 while reconnoitring the French lines at Ticonderoga, Canada, the same summer that Wolfe took Quebec. The sculpture, particularly the bas-relief (by Eckstein) showing Ticonderoga with a skirmish between the French and British was much admired by Flaxman who considered it 'one of the finest productions of art in the Abbey'. The greater part of the monument will be found on the back of the title page.

66   Major John André 1780, P.M. van Gelder (des. Adam) 1821

The son of a Genevese merchant, he was an officer under Sir Henry Clinton in the American War of Independence, and was entrusted with negotiations with the American traitor Benedict Arnold. Returning from a meeting with Arnold behind enemy lines André was captured by American soldiers. Despite the best efforts of the British and the reluctance of George Washington (who is himself depicted in the monument) negotiations failed and André was hanged. The monument depicts him suffering the more honourable military alternative of death by firing squad. After an interval of forty years his remains were transferred to the Abbey with all due ceremony, including a wreath from the Americans. The Lion and Britannia on the title page are also from this monument.

67   Lieutenant-General William Hargrave 1751, Roubiliac c1753

Dismissed by Goldsmith as 'some rich man', popular opinion held that this was the only reason for his memorial in the Abbey. There is little information about him other than that he was 'Governor of Gibraltar'. As with many of Roubiliac's works the reputation of the monument was greater than that of the subject. Hargrave is represented as struggling from a tomb while an angel, above, sounds the last trump and surveys the victory of Time over Death, symbolised by Time snapping Death's dart across his knee; but even as Time triumphs, his own scythe falls from his hand: his reign is over, that of eternity begun. General Conway reported to Horace Walpole the lines scribbled on the monument by a Westminster boy, 'Lie still if you're wise, You'll be damned if you rise,' adding that 'since vice and insignificance have entitled people to an interment in Westminster Abbey, one Gen. Hargraves has slipt in among the crowd'. The obscure significance of the falling pyramid in the background occasionally led the Dean to be reproached for neglecting to repair the monument.

68   Major-General James Fleming 1751, Roubiliac c1751

Like that of his neighbour, General Hargrave [**67**], Fleming's fame does not equal the size of his monument. He was wounded at Blenheim in his youth and for many years commanded the Royal Fusiliers. He was present at the battles of Falkirk and Culloden in the '45 Rebellion and died at Bath. The supporter illustrated is Hercules.

69   Lieutenant-Colonel Sir James Outram 1863, Matthew Noble

Spent most of his life in India as a political and military agent and won the trust and admiration of many, including some of the Indians he was sent to govern. The Amir of Hyderabad confided his brother and son to Outram's protection, on his deathbed. At a dinner in his honour Sir Charles Napier toasted him as 'the Bayard of India, sans peur et sans reproche' and the epithet is used on a marble slab marking his grave in the Abbey's nave. The bas-relief on the monument shows Outram with Generals Campbell and Havelock clasping hands at the relief of the siege of Lucknow during the Indian Mutiny.

70   Dean John Thomas 1793, John Bacon the Younger 1793

Dean of Westminster and Bishop of Rochester, during his time at the Abbey the Choir was refitted and the first Handel festival held. The photograph shows a chalice and what appears to be the communion sacrament in the form of cubes.

71   Dean Joseph Wilcocks 1756, Cheere

Installed Dean of Westminster Abbey in 1731 and on the same day was nominated Bishop of Rochester. He steadily refused further promotion, including the Archbishopric of York, and devoted himself to the Abbey. During his time Hawksmoor's western towers were built; the Dean was so proud of these that he had a bas-relief representing the towers on his monument and lies, as he wished, beneath one of them.

72   Admiral Richard Tyrell 1766, Read 1766

His last and most distinguished deed was the single-handed defeat of three French men-of-war of a much larger fighting strength than his ship the *Buckingham*. It is this incident, which occurred a few months before his death, that is depicted on this controversial monument. However, many contemporary reactions were enthusiastic and Wesley classed it with the Nightingale monument [**30**] by Read's master Roubiliac (for which Read had curved the skeletal figure of Death). The half-naked figure representing Tyrell's soul going up to heaven was removed by Dean Stanley in the nineteenth century who did not concur with those 'persons above the class of rustics' whom he observed admiring the monument.

73   William Congreve 1729, Bird

Dramatist and member of the literary circle surrounding Swift, Pope and Gay. Among his plays were *The Way of the World*, *Love for Love*, and *The Double Dealer*. He also contributed to *The Tatler*. The monument to him was erected by the Duchess of Marlborough with whom he was most intimate in his later life and to whom he left the bulk of his fortune. The portrait medallion is based on a painting by Kneller.

74   Sir Winston Churchill 1965, Reynolds Stone

After the lying-in-state at Westminster Hall Churchill's funeral service was at St Paul's Cathedral. He was buried beside his parents in Bladon churchyard near Blenheim Palace.

75   Henry Fawcett 1884, Sir Alfred Gilbert 1887

A vigorous and enlightened campaigner, he was active in University reforms for dissenters and supported equal rights for women. Despite his total blindness he became a liberal M.P. and helped carry the 1867 Reform Bill. He helped to save Epping Forest from enclosure and also to protect the New Forest. Of the seven Virtues forming the memorial, the central knightly figure of Fortitude, Industry with her beehive, and

Brotherhood with a hoe, are illustrated. This sculpture marks the introduction to Britain of the 'lost wax' method of casting by Gilbert.

76 The Unknown Warrior

The idea of burying an unknown British soldier as a representative of those who died during the First World War, occurred to the Rev David Railton in 1916 while he was serving as a chaplain at the Front. After the War he wrote to the Dean of Westminster and, following a warm response from Lloyd George and Field-Marshal Sir Henry Wilson, King George V overcame his doubts about 'reopening the war wound'. Six working parties were sent to the battlefields of Ypres, the Marne, Cambrai, Arras, the Somme and the Aisne each to exhume the body of one soldier. The remains were examined in an army hut to confirm that they were British and at midnight Brigadier-General Wyatt entered the hut blind-folded and selected by touch one of the coffins. It was placed inside a casket made from a Hampton Court oak tree and taken back to England, escorted by six destroyers. The burial took place on the second anniversary of the Armistice, 11 November 1920; it was reported by *The Times* as 'the most beautiful, the most touching, the most impressive ... the island has ever seen.' The Union Jack that the chaplain had used for burials at the Front was draped over the coffin and now hangs in St George's Chapel. A year later the permanent gravestone of black Belgian marble was unveiled, bearing the inscription shown. As John Betjeman said, the inscription 'must have come from a monumental mason and have been ordered by the foot ... But now I don't know that art is all that important in an inspired idea like this.'

IN OMNIBUS REQUIEM QUÆSIVI

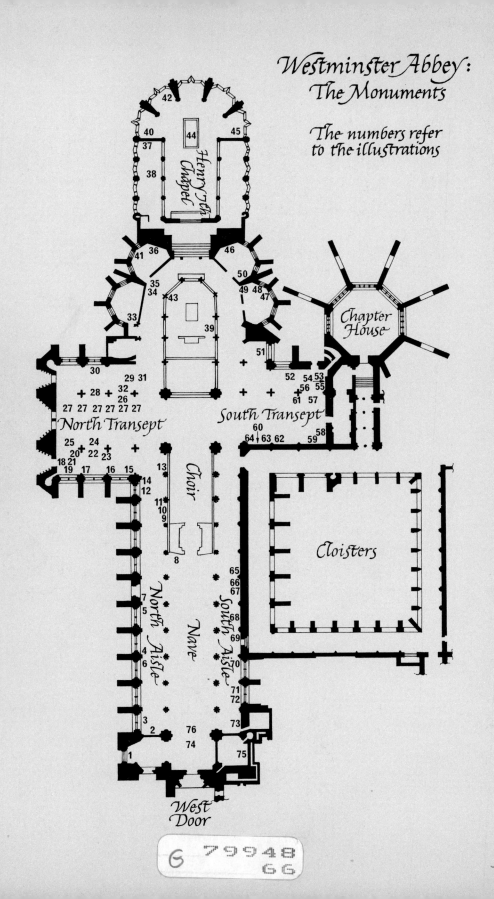

Westminster Abbey:
The Monuments

The numbers refer
to the illustrations

Henry VII Chapel

Chapter House

North Transept

South Transept

Choir

Cloisters

North Aisle

Nave

South Aisle

West Door